ALL ACCESS TAYLOR SWIFT

100% UNOFFICIAL

Emma Carlson Berne

SCHOLASTIC

First published in the UK as *Taylor Swift: All Access* by Scholastic, 2024
This edition published 2025

Scholastic, Bosworth Avenue, Warwick, CV34 6UQ
Scholastic Ireland, 89E Lagan Road, Dublin Industrial Estate, Glasnevin, Dublin, D11 HP5F

First published in the US as *Taylor Swift: All Access* by Scholastic Inc., 2024

PHOTOS ©: Cover center: Kevin Mazur/Getty Images for The Academy hearts: ulimi/DigitalVision Vectors/Getty Images, banner: cnythzl/DigitalVision Vectors/Getty Images, dot pattern: Astrolounge/DigitalVision Vectors/Getty Images, stars: ulimi/DigitalVision Vectors/ Getty Images, dot pattern: vkulieva/iStock/Getty Images. Photo insert: 1: Kevin Mazur/Getty Images for TAS Rights Management, 2 top: Ethan Miller/Getty Images, 2 bottom: Scott Gries/ Getty Images, 3: Rick Diamond/WireImage/Getty Images, 4 top: Christopher Polk/Getty Images, 4 bottom: Kevin Mazur/WireImage/Getty Images, 5 top: Jeff Kravitz/FilmMagic/Getty Images, 5 bottom: Kevin Winter/Getty Images For dcp, 6 top: Kevin Winter/Getty Images for The Recording Academy, 6 bottom: John Shearer/ Getty Images for TAS, 7 top: Kevin Winter/Getty Images for The Recording Academy, 7 bottom: Ezra Shaw/Getty Images, 8: Christopher Polk/Penske Media via Getty Images.

ISBN 978 0702 34918 8

A CIP catalogue record for this book is available from the British Library.

Printed in the UK
Paper made from wood grown in sustainable forests and other controlled sources.

FSC www.fsc.org MIX Paper | Supporting responsible forestry FSC® C018072

10 9 8 7 6 5 4 3 2 1

www.scholastic.co.uk

For safety or quality concerns:
UK: www.scholastic.co.uk/productinformation
EU: www.scholastic.ie/productinformation

TABLE OF CONTENTS

CHAPTER 1

Taylor the World Breaker

She's standing on a huge box on stage in a dark arena. All around her, lights and mobile phones are flashing like a thousand stars. She's wearing a sparkly silver-and-purple bodysuit and glittery knee-high boots. She croons into a mic as giant wall hangings billow around her. When her image flashes on to the jumbo screen behind her, the fans packing the stadium all scream.

She's a megastar. She's Taylor Swift, and she's belting out songs from her album *Lover*.

Her red-lipsticked, cat-eyed face smiles out at her fans from arena stages, album covers and award show red carpets. Swifties know her. Her haters know her. The *world* knows her!

Or do they?

This woman isn't just a musical marvel (one who made $1.82 billion in 2023 – that's right, billion with a *B* – from music, concerts and merch). She's a songwriter, a business and marketing whiz, an ally, a daughter who never leaves her mum behind and most of all, a friend to her fans, who see her as an inspiration.

But Taylor hasn't sailed into the sea of fame without a few storms along the way. She's won 14 Grammys, but she's also been called a snake on social media. She's suffered from depression and bullying. Taylor's watched her mum battle cancer, and she's gone through painful breakups.

From her quiet childhood in Pennsylvania

to her Nashville country music breakthrough, to her stratospheric rise to the pinnacle of musical stardom, Taylor has kept writing, dreaming and fighting.

She's poured her emotions into her music and taken those songs on tour, where she's shared them – and her heart – with her fans.

TAYLOR THE ROYAL RECORD SMASHER

Breaking records is a specialty for Taylor. Here are a few of her most notable smashes:

- She set the record for the most successful music tour ever with the Eras tour. The total earnings? Over a whopping $2 billion!

- Our favourite singer-songwriter also broke the record for the most Grammys for Album of the Year when she won her fourth award for *Midnights* at the 2024 Grammys. The previous record holders, who each won three times, were Paul Simon, Frank Sinatra and Stevie Wonder – all men, in case you didn't notice.

- She was the youngest person ever to win the Country Music Association Award for Entertainer of the Year. That was in 2009, when Taylor was 19.

- The winner of the most American Music Awards? Oh, Taylor Swift. She has 40! Her closest competitors are Michael Jackson and Whitney Houston, with 26 and 22, respectively.

- And of course, no other female musician in the industry earns more than Taylor. She tops the list with her net worth (how much money she has) at an estimated $1.6 billion (again with those *B*'s). Rake it in, Taylor!

- Taylor has smashed records before, of course – in 2010, she became the youngest singer ever to win Album of the Year at the Grammys, for *Fearless*.

TAYLOR'S ERAS

Welcome to Swiftie U

Already have a degree in Taylor Swift-ology? Enrol in Swiftie University and get ready for your PhD!

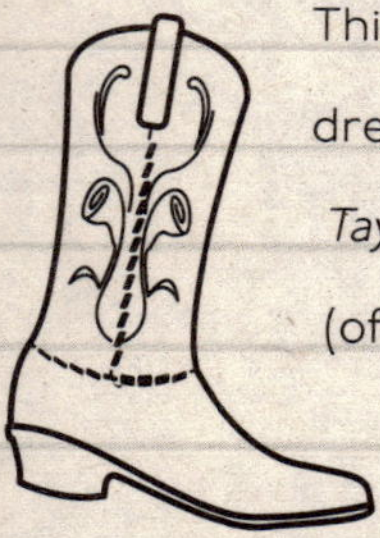

Young Taylor released ***Taylor Swift*** as her debut in 2006. The album included hit single, 'Tim McGraw'. This era (2006–2008) is all about Taylor's curls, flowing dresses, ruffles, cowboy boots and sweetness. *Taylor Swift* also won the singer her first Grammy (of many to come) for Best New Artist.

In the ***Fearless*** era (2008–2010), Taylor started moving away from country towards pop, with sparkly dresses, fringe and ball gowns as she sang about the highs and lows of love and heartbreak. Taylor won four Grammys for *Fearless*, including Album of the Year (she later rerecorded the album in 2021). On tour, Taylor would perform songs from this album while standing in front of a sparkly, fairy tale castle.

Taylor penned the songs on ***Speak Now*** (2010–2012) solo, clapping back at criticism that she didn't write her own songs. She originally released this record – her third era – in 2010, earning herself two Grammys. She showed off her grown-up aesthetic on tour with plenty of purple and glam metallic dresses with fringe. She also released her first perfume, *Wonderstruck*, which came in a purple bottle. Taylor rerecorded *Speak Now* in July 2023.

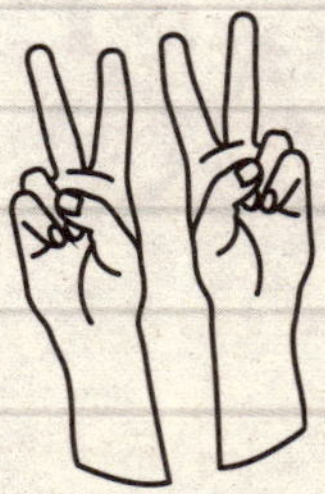

Red is Taylor's 2012 album release and fourth era. She described this album as representing a heartbroken person, a puzzle of scattered pieces that all fit together in the end. Taylor's tour look for this era (2012–2014) was experimental, with lots of high-waisted shorts and vintage dresses, paired with red lipstick and a fringe haircut. She rerecorded *Red* in November 2021.

Taylor earned three Grammys, including her second Album of the Year, for ***1989***, which she originally released in 2014 and rerecorded in October 2023. This era (2014–2016) marked Taylor's entrance into pop superstardom, and her tour look matched, with edgy bustiers, sequined jumpsuits, crop tops, bobbed hair and skater skirts. Taylor rocked all the award shows and stages during this era, and absolutely everyone knew who she was.

reputation was Taylor's 2017–2018 era answer to critics both online and IRL. She showed the world she was tough with black catsuits, leather, dark lipstick and lots of snake imagery during concerts.

Taylor switched from darkness to light two years later when she released ***Lover*** (2019). This album is all about butterflies, rainbows, pastels and love! Her multicoloured tour was cut short by the COVID-19 pandemic, but Taylor still had time during this era (2019–2020) to signal her stance as an ally for the LGBTQ+ community.

folklore was Taylor's COVID lockdown project and 2020 release. This album is different from Taylor's previous records – more folk songs, more indie-rock than pop, more storytelling – and plenty of summer romance. Taylor's era (2020–2021) aesthetic for *folklore* was all cosy cardigans and dresses, plaid, velvet and loose buns and braids. *folklore* won Taylor her third Album of the Year Grammy.

Taylor described ***evermore***, which also came out in 2020, as the sister album to *folklore*. This record is also all about folk songs, with a hefty dash of a spooky, elegant look – think gothic forests in winter complete with velvet capes with hoods.

Midnights, which Taylor released in 2022, swings back to the darker side of life. Taylor has said she wrote these songs during many sleepless nights, exploring feelings of longing, separation and loneliness. Taylor embraces seventies fashion for this era's space-era, sky-bound aesthetic.

The Tortured Poets Department, Taylor's eleventh original album, released in April 2024. The aesthetics of this era was influenced by dark academia and gothic literature like Frankenstein. Taylor wore a lot of dark colours, preppy outfits and lace during this era.

The Life of the Showgirl was Taylor's twelfth album released on October 2025 and marked the start of a new era. The pop sound was brought to life with a lot of sparkly outfits , feathers and Taylor's signature red lipstick.

CHAPTER 2

A Star Is Born

When Taylor Alison Swift was born on December 13, 1989, her mum and dad didn't want to give her just any name. First of all, they wanted her to have a name that could be a boy's name or a girl's name. That way, they thought, she wouldn't be held back by any gender stereotypes. Andrea and Scott Swift were going to give their new little daughter every chance they could.

And how about a name inspired by music? After all, Andrea's mother had a career as an international opera singer. Music was in this new little baby's veins. *Taylor*, Andrea and Scott decided, after one of their favourite folk singers, James Taylor.

Taylor's dad was a investment manager, so little Taylor just assumed that she'd be in business when she grew up. But words and performing have always called to Taylor, even when she was a little girl. She listened to a LeAnn Rimes CD on repeat and loved writing poetry – she even won a national poetry contest – and she loved acting and singing in local children's theatre productions. She played Maria in *The Sound of Music* and Sandy in *Grease*.

When Taylor's parents realized how much their daughter loved singing and performing, they started taking nine-year-old Taylor for regular acting and voice lessons in New York City. Soon, Taylor started dreaming of Broadway. She had to auditions for different parts. Later, Taylor remembered how *tall* (she's five foot eleven inches) she felt, standing with the other girls in the corridors, waiting to be called in.

But soon, Taylor and her parents realized that Broadway wasn't the place for her. She wasn't getting parts. That was okay – Taylor was growing up and figuring out even more of what she really wanted. And she was starting a serious love affair with country music.

For Taylor, singing country was all about the storytelling, every song was like a new story. She loved country stars Shania Twain and Faith Hill. And seeing her opera singer grandmother get up in church every week and belt out hymns showed Taylor that singing on stage could be, well, *fun*.

Sing, Sing, Sing!

Taylor's family moved to a wealthy suburb

called Wyomissing, near Reading, and Taylor started singing all the time. She sang karaoke and recorded herself. She got her mum to take her to karaoke competitions. She dragged her parents to every country music festival and fair she could find.

One night in Reading, Taylor took her first sip of fame. She was at the local Reading Fightin' Phils baseball game, along with the rest of the children's theatre cast of *Grease*. The game was having a 1950s theme night and the cast was going to sing some songs on the field before the game began. Just before the start of the game, the manager realized that the person who was scheduled to sing the anthem hadn't shown up. Maybe ... Taylor could do it? Taylor and her mum looked at each other. Maybe she could.

Quickly, Taylor rehearsed the song with her mum, then ran out on to the field. She belted out the anthem and the crowd screamed with appreciation. Later in the season, she came back to perform again, then at other sports games, and gradually, people began realizing that this girl had a *voice*.

Soon, other people were realizing the same thing. When the organizers at the Philadelphia 76ers realized they needed another anthem singer, they called the kid they'd heard about from nearby Wyomissing. They booked her to sing and on April 5, 2002, the announcer asked the audience to welcome "Taylor Swift from Reading, PA." A twelve-year-old Taylor, in a red cardigan and a headband holding back her long blonde hair, grasped the microphone and sang the national anthem to a cheering crowd, grinning the whole time. Taylor was doing what she loved most and she was just getting started.

CHAPTER 3

"Hi! I'm Taylor!"

Taylor wanted to be a country music singer, and she knew as well as anyone there was just one place to be: Nashville. The Nashville country music scene had nurtured famous singers like Dolly Parton, Carrie Underwood, Garth Brooks and Hank Williams. The recording studios and stages of Nashville had launched a thousand country careers, and Taylor was determined to be the thousandth and first.

When she was eleven, Taylor convinced

TAYLOR'S COSIEST CHRISTMAS MEMORIES

Lots of people love Christmas.
But you know who *really* loves Christmas?
That's right! Our very own T. A. Swift!

- Taylor's always excited for autumn because it means Christmas is right around the corner. Her friends even tease her that she's actually an elf – that's how much she loves Christmas.

- Taylor makes her own snow globes for Christmas gifts. She uses mason jars, glitter and antique Christmas ornaments.

☆ Even though she's a megastar, Taylor always tries to remember what her friends might want for Christmas. All year long, if a friend mentions something she might like, Taylor whips out her phone and writes it down then and there.

☆ In 2014, Taylor sent customized Christmas gifts to thirty-two especially chosen fans around the world in an event known as 'Swiftmas'. These stuffed FedEx boxes included candles, cameras and film, gift cards, jumpers and scatter cushions. Taylor even helped one fan pay off her student loans. Merry Swiftmas, everyone!

☆ Like lots of us, Taylor gets into the Christmas spirit by listening to her favourite holiday songs. She loves Bing Crosby, Mariah Carey's 'All I Want for Christmas Is You,' the Beach Boys' Christmas songs and Fountains of Wayne's 'Valley Winter Song' – which isn't exactly a Christmas song (except it is to Taylor).

TAYLOR'S INSPIRATIONAL ICONS

Taylor often talks about the musicians and songwriters who have inspired her, from an old-school Beatle to a queen of country.

☆ Folk singer Joni Mitchell's songwriting has long been an influence on Taylor. She's said that Mitchell's album *Blue* is one of her favourites.

☆ Taylor finds inspiration in punk band Fall Out Boy's lyrics. She collaborated with the band on her *Speak Now* rerecord. Meanwhile, Fall Out Boy's bassist and lyricist, Pete Wentz, has called Taylor "breathtaking".

☆ Paul McCartney has long been one of Taylor's favourite musicians – and not just for his legendary music. She has said that she also admires his personal kindness and selflessness as a performer.

☆ One of Taylor's earliest influences is still one of her strongest – country music legend Shania Twain. And the admiration goes both ways; in 2023, when Taylor wore a T-shirt that referenced Shania's song 'Any Man of Mine', Shania said how much she respects Taylor and her hard work.

☆ Taylor has long given the country music trio the Chicks credit for inspiring her music. She's even said that the first song she learned on guitar was a Chicks tune called 'Cowboy Take Me Away'. In 2019, Taylor and the Chicks released a collaboration – the song 'Soon You'll Get Better', on *Lover*, which references Taylor's mother's battle with cancer.

Andrea to fly with her down to Nashville, and there, with a demo CD of herself singing Chicks and Dolly Parton, she started knocking on doors while her mum and her little brother waited in the car. Every time a music executive answered, she would hand them the CD and say, "Hi! I'm Taylor! I want a record deal."

But Taylor didn't get a record deal. No one wanted to sign an eleven-year-old singing covers. But maybe, she thought, they'd sign an eleven-year-old singing her *own* songs and playing guitar.

Taylor Goes to Work

Taylor and her mum went back to Pennsylvania, and Taylor went to work. She picked up a guitar and started teaching herself to play. And as she learned chords and music notes, the words to songs started coming as well. Soon, songwriting became a break from the drama of school. She couldn't wait to get home and write every afternoon.

Taylor's fingers cracked and bled from playing her twelve-string guitar four hours a day. On the weekends, she played for six hours a day! Her mum would tape up her fingers and Taylor would keep going. She never wanted to stop.

Soon, she had enough material for a new demo CD – this one of herself, playing her own songs. Taylor went back to Nashville and handed out her demo again. This time, the music executives noticed. Taylor landed a record deal with RCA.

Taylor had her record deal. But she wanted more. Her label wanted her to record other people's music as well as her own.

And Taylor had decided long ago that she only wanted to record her own songs.

So Taylor decided to switch labels. She met with an executive at the Sony record label, and when he heard her play a few of her songs on guitar, he knew he had found a star. He offered Taylor a recording deal, making her the youngest songwriter the label had ever signed.

Now Taylor was living a different life than her friends in year eight. They were going to secondary school, and she was cutting her debut record album. While her friends were going to sports practice after school, Taylor's mum was driving her to songwriting sessions with professional writers. There, Taylor was learning all about how to craft hit country songs – lessons that she wasn't ever going to forget. Taylor knew that if she wanted to make it big in country music, she was going to need to leave Pennsylvania. It was time to move to Nashville. Taylor's parents agreed. Leaving Pennsylvania was a big change, but Taylor's music career was taking off. They needed to support her.

Nashville Party

Taylor's parents sold their house in Pennsylvania and moved everyone to a house on a lake in Hendersonville, Tennessee, just outside Nashville. Taylor went to work with Liz Rose, her songwriting partner. One day, when Taylor was sitting in maths class, she started thinking of a guy she knew who had moved away. She was making a mental list of things that reminded her of him – and one was a song by the country singer, Tim McGraw.

Taylor ran home from school, sat down at the piano stand with Liz, wrote the song 'Tim McGraw' in about fifteen minutes.

Taylor flew into the world and embraced it, leaving high school behind and switching to homeschooling so she could tour and promote her album. She did her homework in the back seat of rental cars and on the floor of airport lounges. She went from radio station to radio station, talking about her album and staying at cheap hotels every night.

Taylor was working hard and she was loving every minute of it. She was making music, making records and most of all, making her dreams come true.

CHAPTER 4

That Night at the VMAs

Taylor's hard work was paying off. In 2007, she stood on the stage at the Country Music Association (CMA) Awards in a gold ball gown. Her wavy, blonde hair was looped up softly at the back of her head, and big sparkly earrings dangled from her ears. She already looked like a star, and the CMA agreed that she was on her way to becoming one.

That night, she accepted the Horizon Award, which was meant for rising stars in the country music industry. It was Taylor's first major music

OUTRAGEOUS OUTFITS

Taylor's outfits. Taylor's outfits! Shimmering in fringes, posing in frothy ball gowns, keeping it casual in her favourite high-waisted shorts – she always looks fabulous.

- Taylor always shimmers, but she really shone in the pink crystal-studded Versace bodysuit she wore with matching over-the-knee sparkly boots on the South American leg of her Eras tour. She's also donned this now-iconic bodysuit in pink and blue, as well as gold and silver.

- While performing 'Shake It Off' in 2014, and possibly inspired by the flappers of the 1920s, Taylor wore a white fringed crop top and skirt, decorated with Swarovski crystals.

- Pretty in purple at the 2008 Country Music Association Awards, Taylor wore a violet silk gown with a glittery headband, perfect for performing her fairy tale ballad, 'Love Story.'

- The blue, sweeping ball gown Taylor wore during the Eras tour while playing songs from *Speak Now* was fit for a princess – or pop princess, as in this case.

- Taylor kept it simple in 2012 when she wore a red-and-white-striped tee, black high-waisted shorts and bright red loafers to sing 'We Are Never Ever Getting Back Together'.

- Tough in black leather, Taylor showed off in a tight black catsuit with cutouts during the 1989 tour in 2015.

- Taylor showed the world she wasn't afraid of being bold when she put on the short, A-line red dress for her performance of 'You Belong with Me' at the 2009 MTV Awards – right after Kanye West stole her microphone.

TAYLOR'S WILDEST FAN-TASIES

Swifties, you know who you are. And you know how much Taylor loves you. Here's a few of the most fabulous fan moments:

- In 2018, Taylor put her well-known generosity on display when she donated $10,000 to help Jacob, a young fan with autism, get a service dog. But Taylor didn't stop there. She also invited Jacob and his dog, Reid, to a Reputation concert in Houston. She met the pair backstage, where she gave them both big hugs.

- Even Taylor herself was in the background when two fans got engaged right in front of her at a 2018 Reputation tour stop. The couple revealed that they'd met five years prior at a Red concert.

When a seven-year-old named Bella handed a fan letter to an usher before an Eras show, she and her mom thought they'd never hear back. But not only did Taylor receive the letter backstage, she also autographed it, then sent a crew member to find Bella at her seat and deliver it back to her.

One couple wanted to bring their own love story to an Arizona Eras tour show and decided to get married during a break in the set! They brought their own officiant, witnesses and bridal party – and of course, a white dress.

Sometimes, even Taylor herself gets carried away. When she saw a particularly adorable fan at a Chicago Eras show, she wanted to bring her on stage. Taylor gently grasped the little girl's arm to help her get up on to the stage, but then she realized that she didn't have a safe way to get her *off* the stage. So, she gave the little girl a big high-five instead.

FUN FACT

On June 19, 2006, 'Tim McGraw' was released as Taylor's debut single. The video won Taylor a Country Music Television (CMT) Award for Breakthrough Video of the Year in 2007. On October 24, 2006, sixteen-year-old Taylor Swift was officially introduced to the world when her first album, *Taylor Swift*, was released in North America, with 'Tim McGraw' as the first track. World, meet Taylor.

award, and it was given in honour of the success of 'Tim McGraw' and *Taylor Swift*. Taylor had tears in her eyes as she accepted the award. She thanked her family for moving to Nashville and the music business for believing in her. And most of all, she thanked her fans for changing her life forever. It was, she said, the highlight of her senior year.

Taylor's Fearless

But this moment was far from Taylor's peak. In fact, she was just getting started. One year later, on November 11, 2008, Taylor released her second album, *Fearless*, which climbed the charts to become her first number one record. It spent eleven weeks topping the Billboard 200, and it would go on to become the bestselling album of 2009 *and* win Taylor her first Album of the Year Grammy.

This was Taylor's breakthrough moment.

She was crossing over from country to pop with her sweet, soulful love song, 'You Belong with Me,' which was paired with a rom-com-worthy video featuring Taylor in two roles – the kind, nerdy girl-next-door, and the villainous, dark-haired cheerleader.

Taylor was living her own kind of fairy tale. But she didn't know that her story was about to have its first big twist.

VMA Surprise

At the 2009 MTV Video Music Awards, the Award for Best Female Video was announced. Taylor had won! Lots of other talented musicians had been nominated, too – Kelly Clarkson, P!nk, Lady Gaga, Katy Perry ... and Beyoncé!

The cameras flashed on Taylor's excited face in the audience as she rose from her seat and made her way to the podium in a long silver column dress. On stage, she was surrounded by the presenters and handed the little Moonman (now referred to as Moon Person) that was her award. Smiling and breathless, Taylor took the microphone. "Thank you so much!" she began. "I always dreamt about what it would be like to maybe win one of these someday."

But before Taylor could finish her speech, someone else was on stage – the rapper, Kanye West, who had come up through the audience. He plucked the microphone from Taylor's surprised hand. "Yo, Taylor," he said. "I'm really happy for you. I'mma let you finish. But Beyoncé had one of the best videos of *all time*!"

What was happening? The cameras flashed quickly on to Beyoncé's shocked face in the audience. "Oh, Kanye," she said.

On stage, Taylor didn't know what to do. Kanye still had the microphone. "One of the best videos of all time!" Kanye said again. Then he shrugged a little and handed the microphone back to Taylor.

The crowd had no idea what to do. They had cheered for an instant when Kanye said Beyoncé's name, but now, they started booing.

Taylor stood alone on stage, clutching her award and the microphone. The booing got louder and louder.

Taylor had no idea what to do. What had just happened? Who were they booing? Were they booing *her*? Her fairy tale world was crashing down. Taylor didn't know what to say. She didn't say anything.

Backstage, Taylor rushed into her mother's arms and sobbed. Her team surrounded her. Did the audience all agree with Kanye? Did they all hate her?

But Taylor couldn't keep crying. She couldn't hide. She had to perform 'You Belong with Me' in front of that same audience in about five minutes.

Taylor knew something terrible had happened, but she also knew that she wasn't going to let a bully take more than one more minute of her spotlight. She wiped off her face, changed into a short, bright-red dress, and right on cue, she headed back out.

CHAPTER 5

Triumph and Worries

When Beyoncé got up on stage later to accept her award for Video of the Year, she asked Taylor to come back up and finish her acceptance speech. Taylor did, but she was shaken. Support poured in, with stars like Katy Perry and Kelly Clarkson tweeting that Kanye had been wrong. Even then-president Barack Obama said that Kanye had misbehaved.

Kanye knew he had messed up. He told late-night host Jay Leno that he wanted to apologize to Taylor, and later, Taylor said that he had indeed called her to say he was sorry. The support she'd got from other musicians and from her fans helped her to accept his apology, she said. Otherwise, she wasn't sure she could have.

Solace in Songwriting

But even with Kanye's apology, Taylor was struggling to put the incident behind her – so she did what she's always done to grapple with her feelings. She sat down to write. In 2010, after the release of *Speak Now*, Taylor was back on stage at the VMAs. But this time, she held on to her own microphone as she performed 'Innocent,' a song about Kanye. "Thirty-two and still growin' up now," Taylor sang. "Who you are is not what you did." While she played, clips of the incident unspooled on the huge screens behind her.

A KITTY-CAT CRASH COURSE

Taylor loves her kitties. She has three: Meredith Grey (named after a character on the TV show *Grey's Anatomy*), Benjamin Button (named after the character in the movie *The Curious Case of Benjamin Button*) and Olivia Benson (named after a character on *Law & Order: SVU*). Read on for a few fun kitty-cat facts:

- Taylor hates leaving her cats behind. When she travels on tour, she sometimes brings one of them in a special rucksack. It has a little bubble so the cat can see out.

- The cats showed up in Taylor's 2020 holiday card. They wore winter accessories and posed against a background that recalled Taylor's 2020 album *folklore*.

☆ When Taylor had her picture taken as *Time* magazine's 2023 Person of the Year, Benjamin Button appeared in the photo with her, draped over her shoulders like a furry stole.

☆ Meredith and Olivia are both a type of cat called a Scottish fold. Their ears are naturally folded over, giving them a distinct smush-eared look.

☆ Benjamin Button, on the other hand, has stand-up cat ears, along with blue eyes. He's a breed called a Ragdoll, which is known for being sweet-natured and easy to get along with.

☆ Taylor adopted Benjamin after she met him on the set of a video shoot. Benjamin was just supposed to appear in the video – but he ended up going home with his new mum.

FEARLESS ON THE AWARDS STAGE

Taylor is at home on the awards stage – she has to be, since she seems to spend half her life up there! Check out these highlights:

- One of Taylor's best award show moments was also one of her first. Clad in a gold ball gown, Taylor accepted the Horizon Award from the Country Music Association, given out to rising musicians. She told the crowd, "This is definitely the highlight of my senior year."

- Taylor's won 14 Grammys and been nominated 52 times, but her very first Grammy was in 2010 when she took home, not one, but *four* golden gramophones for Best Country Song ('White Horse'), Best Country Album (*Fearless*), Best Female Country Vocal Performance ('White Horse', again) and Album of the Year (*Fearless*, again).

☆ At the 2019 American Music Awards, Taylor previewed her Eras skills when she performed a compilation of past hits before accepting the award for Artist of the Decade.

☆ Taylor stepped out of the musical arena and into the political one at the 2018 American Music Awards. Clad in a tight, mirrored dress and holding her Artist of the Year award, she urged everyone watching to get out and vote in the upcoming mid-term elections.

☆ Taylor got more personal than usual at the 2021 Grammys. Wearing a flowered mini-dress, Taylor accepted the award for Album of the Year (for *folklore*), and thanked her then-boyfriend Joe Alwyn as the first person she played every song for.

☆ Taylor brought a lot of dates to the 2015 MTV VMAs – her glamorous "squad" of friends, including models Gigi Hadid and Cara Delevingne, and singer and actor Selena Gomez.

☆ At the 2024 Grammys, while accepting the award for Best Pop Vocal Album for *Midnights*, Taylor dropped another bomb on the audience when she announced her newest album, *The Tortured Poets Department*, to be released later in the year. That was the same night Taylor won a fourth Album of the Year award, this time for *Midnights*, setting a new record for most wins!

Taylor's fame kept rising. *Red* was released in 2012, and in 2015, her 1989 world tour broke the record for the highest grossing U.S. tour by a female artist. She even got a chance to clap back at Kanye a little. When she presented him with the Video Vanguard Award at the 2015 VMAs, Taylor told him, "I'm really happy for you and I'm going to let you finish, but Kanye West has had one of the greatest careers of all time." Afterwards, Kanye sent her flowers. From the outside, it seemed like Taylor's fairy tale life was back on track.

Real Problems

But inside, Taylor had a new worry. In 2015, her mum, Andrea, who is also her best friend, was diagnosed with breast cancer. Taylor had told Andrea she wanted her to get screened for Christmas, as a present to her kids, and the tests revealed cancer. Taylor posted about her mum's diagnosis on her Tumblr and asked her fans for support. Later, Andrea's breast cancer came back, and she was also diagnosed with a brain tumor. Taylor wrote about how much she would miss her mum if anything happened to her. "What am I supposed to do / If there's no you?" Taylor sang in 'Soon You'll Get Better', on 2019's *Lover*.

"[My mum's cancer has] taught me that there are real problems and then there's everything else. My mum's cancer is a real problem. I used to be so anxious about daily ups and downs. I give all of my worry, stress, and prayers to real problems now," Taylor told *Elle* magazine.

But even though Taylor knew nothing was more important than her mum's health, she still couldn't shed her problems with Kanye. In 2016, Kanye released his song 'Famous', which referred to Taylor in rude words and

TAYLOR IN HER NOW-ICONIC PINK-AND-BLUE BODYSUIT AT THE OPENING NIGHT OF THE ERAS TOUR IN GLENDALE, ARIZONA

★ A *FEARLESS*-ERA TAYLOR SHOWS HER COUNTRY-MUSIC ROOTS WITH SOFT RINGLETS AND A SPARKLY GUITAR.

★ TAYLOR IS THRILLED AT HER FIRST MAJOR MUSIC AWARD, GIVEN AT THE 2007 CMAS.

TAYLOR'S VIOLET BALL GOWN WAS PERFECT FOR HER PERFORMANCE OF "LOVE STORY" AT THE 2008 CMAS.

★ TAYLOR'S ACCEPTANCE SPEECH AT THE 2009 VMAS WAS INTERRUPTED BY RAPPER KANYE WEST.

★ TAYLOR WENT CASUAL AT THE 2012 VMAS DURING HER PERFORMANCE OF "WE ARE NEVER EVER GETTING BACK TOGETHER."

★ TAYLOR AND HER "SQUAD" SMILE AT THE 2015 VMAS.

★ SEQUINED AND SMILING AT THE 2018 AMAS, TAYLOR URGES HER FANS TO REGISTER TO VOTE.

TAYLOR THANKS HER THEN-BOYFRIEND JOE ALWYN AFTER HER 2021 ALBUM OF THE YEAR WIN FOR *FOLKLORE*.

TAYLOR POSES WITH BEYONCÉ AT THE PREMIERE OF THE ERAS TOUR CONCERT FILM.

TAYLOR HOLDS HER FOURTH ALBUM OF THE YEAR AWARD AT THE 2024 GRAMMYS.

TAYLOR CELEBRATES BOYFRIEND TRAVIS KELCE'S SUPER BOWL LVIII WIN ON THE FIELD IN LAS VEGAS.

TAYLOR'S FUTURE ERAS ARE SURE TO BE EXCITING AS SHE CONTINUES BREAKING RECORDS AND SOARING TO NEW HEIGHTS.

claimed that he had made her famous by insulting her. Whatever reconciliation Taylor and Kanye had was over. Taylor was horrified. But Kanye insisted that he'd received permission from Taylor ahead of time to use her name in his song. Taylor said this was not true.

The argument with Kanye got worse when Kanye's wife, Kim Kardashian, released a series of videos that claimed to show Kanye talking to Taylor on the phone and asking her permission to talk about her in his song. In the videos, Taylor seemed to agree. But the videos were edited, so it was not clear what exactly she is agreeing to.

Taylor, Kanye and Kim were mixed up in a big, public argument – a feud. Even though fans were flooding Taylor with support, she was also getting backlash. Online, Kim called Taylor a snake, and soon, Kim's fans joined in, flooding social media with snake emojis.

It was one of the lowest points of Taylor's career. She had to get away to protect herself. And so, in mid-2016, Taylor dropped out of sight. She even moved out of the United States for a little while. She rented a house, stopped posting on social media and stayed in. She pushed away her friends and didn't know who she could trust any more.

CHAPTER 6

The Snake Bites Back

Then, in August 2017, Taylor suddenly showed up. She deleted all her old social media posts. She posted a picture of a snake on all her accounts. She was about to announce something big, her fans speculated.

They were right. On August 23, 2017, Taylor broke her silence. She announced that her new album, *reputation*, would be dropping in November, and with that, she burst back on to the world stage. But this time, Taylor was taking charge of the story. That snake?

That symbol was hers now.

Taylor put the snake on her concert merch and in her videos. During her Reputation tour, Taylor floated over her fans' heads in a snake-shaped cage. Three giant snakes, including a 19-metre blow-up cobra named Karyn shared the stage with Taylor as she belted out her songs holding a gold snake microphone. "So you're wondering why there are so many snakes on stage, right?" Taylor asked the crowd during her opening night concert in Glendale, Arizona, on May 8, 2018. She was laughing in the face of her haters, and more than that, she was telling her fans that bullying doesn't have to defeat you. It can make you stronger.

Fans Forever

And Taylor wasn't defeated. *reputation* was the top selling album of 2017, even though it

FUN FACT

When she isn't writing songs, recording or performing, Taylor is also an actor and director! She has appeared in several shows and movies including *Valentine's Day*, *Cats*, *New Girl* and *CSI: Crime Scene Investigation*. She also directed a short film for the ten-minute version of her song, 'All Too Well,' as well as many of her music videos.

TAYLOR'S TIDBITS

Speaking her mind is another Taylor talent. She tells the truth, and she doesn't hold back.

- "If I'm gonna write songs about my exes, they can write songs about me. That's how it works."
- "When we're falling in love or out of it, that's when we most need a song that says how we feel."
- "Being fearless isn't being 100 per cent not fearful; it's being terrified but you jump anyway."
- "No matter what happens in life, be good to people. Being good to people is a wonderful legacy to leave behind."
- "I love having a goal, feeling like I'm on a mission. I love trying to beat what I've done so far."

didn't release until November, moving more than one million copies in the first week alone. Taylor was getting smarter about her public image, too. She started posting less on social media. She answered fewer questions from the press. She didn't want to get hurt again. But she didn't pull away from her fans. After all, she credits them with getting her through her low times. "The fans and their care for me, my well-being and my music were the ones who pulled me through," Taylor told *Elle* magazine. "The most emotional part of the reputation Stadium Tour for me was knowing I was looking out at the faces of the people who helped me get back up. I'll never forget the ones who stuck around."

CHAPTER 7

Taylor Helps

Taylor had long stayed away from politics, but in 2018, in the lead-up to the mid-term elections, Taylor broke her silence on Democrat vs. Republican, and came out in support of Tennessee Democrats, Phil Bredesen and Jim Cooper. But Taylor didn't stop there. She also spoke out against Tennessee Republican Congresswoman, Marsha Blackburn, and her voting record on protections for women and the LGBTQ+ community. Taylor wrote,

"So many intelligent, thoughtful and self-possessed people have turned 18 in the past two years and now have the right and privilege to make their vote count. But first you need to register, which is quick and easy to do".

And Taylor's fans heard her. Her post got over 2 million likes, and 48 hours after she posted, about 169,000 new voters registered through the voter registration site Taylor had recommended.

LUCKY THIRTEEN

Taylor has always been obsessed with the number thirteen. It's her lucky number and it shows up over and over in her life, including:

- Taylor was born on December 13.
- She was thirteen when she got her first record development deal.
- During shows early in her career, Taylor would draw a thirteen on her hands.
- In 2006, Taylor's first album *Taylor Swift*, went gold in thirteen weeks.
- 'Our Song', her first number one hit, has a thirteen-second intro.
- In 2018, Taylor won thirteen awards.

- She's won a lot of her awards at shows where she's seated in the thirteenth row.
- Taylor's concert movie, *Taylor Swift: The Eras Tour*, released on October 13.
- On X, formerly Twitter, Taylor's account ends in thirteen.
- Versions of *Fearless*, *1989* and *Midnights* each have thirteen tracks.
- On *Red*, the thirteenth song is titled 'The Lucky One'.
- In 2024, Taylor won her thirteenth Grammy.
- The LVIII Super Bowl was Taylor's thirteenth Kansas City Chiefs game – which she attended to cheer on her boyfriend, Travis Kelce!

TAYLOR'S NIBBLY NOSHES

Taylor's said that after a run of shows, she has all her meals in bed – perhaps including one of these delicious dishes?

- Taylor makes tasty homemade cinnamon rolls with icing, which she sometimes brings in to share with her boyfriend, Travis Kelce, and his teammates.

- In the past, Taylor's Starbucks order was a skinny vanilla latte on weekdays and a pumpkin spice latte for weekends. In 2021, she took her love affair with Starbucks a little further and debuted her updated fave drink, a grande caramel nonfat latte. Starbucks even called the beverage, 'Taylor's Latte'. One to go, please!

- Her drive-through order? A cheeseburger, chips and a chocolate shake.

- Taylor often fuels up on concert days with a hearty breakfast of eggs, scones and sausage.

- She'd eat chicken tenders every day if she could.

- Taylor also loves to cook for the people she loves. Her friend Gigi Hadid – who is a supermodel – says that Taylor makes great Bolognese sauce for spaghetti, and fantastic chilli. Taylor also likes to make meatballs, the Indian dish Mughlai chicken and chicken fajitas with *mole* (that's a dark Mexican sauce). *Yum!*

Offering a Hand to Others

Taylor also uses her influence to promote up-and-coming musicians – just like she was, once. She invited artists like singer-songwriters Maisie Peters, Gracie Abrams and GAYLE to open for her on the Eras tour, knowing that Taylor-level exposure could launch their careers. During an Eras show in Sydney, Australia, Taylor even rescued her friend and fellow singer, Sabrina Carpenter, after Sabrina's opening act was cancelled due to bad weather. The show was late getting started, but that didn't stop Taylor from bringing Sabrina up on stage with her to sing a duet instead.

Taylor's always been an ally to the LGBTQ+ community as well.

"Why are you mad?" Taylor sings in "You Need to Calm Down", from *Lover*. "When you could be GLAAD? (You could be GLAAD)." GLAAD is a nonprofit organization that focuses on the representation of LGBTQ+ people in the media and entertainment, and Taylor has long been a donor and a supporter. The video for the song featured Taylor with an array of LGBTQ+ entertainers and activists. During Pride month in June, Taylor told the crowds at a Chicago Eras show that her arenas were safe spaces for LGBTQ+ people, and she supports voting against legislation that chips away at LGBTQ+ rights.

As a Nashville musician through and through, Taylor has also made sure that young music lovers can learn about the culture of country music at the Taylor Swift Education Centre, which is housed at the Country Music Hall of Fame and Museum in Nashville. The centre displays

FUN FACT

Taylor's fans listen when she sings, but they also listen when she *speaks*. In 2023, *Forbes* magazine ranked Taylor as the fifth most powerful woman on the planet (behind the European Commission president, the European Central Bank president, Vice President Kamala Harris and the Italian prime minister!) Taylor feels a responsibility to use her giant platform for the causes that she feels are important.

student art inspired by country music, holds instrument and songwriting workshops and camps, and offers school trips and school programmes. She often donates her used guitars so that non-profits can auction them off to raise money. One of her autographed guitars, decorated with art from the *evermore* album, raised $25,000 for an organization that provides addiction services and financial counselling for people in the music industry.

Feed the World

And Taylor's reach extends to ordinary people in the cities she visits. During the Eras tour, Taylor would often make a hefty donation to a food bank in the city in which she was playing. In Arizona, she donated so much money to a food bank network that the organization was able to send out several lorries full of fresh fruits and vegetables. When Taylor donates and talks about hunger on stage, other people listen, too. Donations to food banks in the city go up.

Taylor doesn't forget the people who work for her, either – after the Eras tour made more money than anticipated, She gave $100,000 bonuses to her tour lorry drivers. Since she has about 50 drivers, the total was about $5 million!

And she's there for the sad times, too. When a shooting broke out at the Kansas City Chiefs 2024 Super Bowl victory parade, Taylor gave $100,000 to a GoFundMe set up for Lisa Lopez-Galvan, a radio DJ killed at the event – showing once again that this megastar knows how to spread love, both on stage and off.

CHAPTER 8

A Taylor Era

In 2019, Taylor found herself with a brand new problem. She had recorded her first six albums (*Taylor Swift*, *Fearless*, *Red*, *Speak Now*, *1989* and *reputation*) with Big Machine Records. Recently, Big Machine had sold the rights to these albums to a music manager named Scooter Braun. This meant that Scooter now owned the master recordings of these albums – the original recordings – and anytime someone wanted to play one of these songs, for a movie or a

TV show, for instance, *he* would make money, not Taylor.

To make matters worse, Taylor felt Scooter had bullied her for years. She was furious. She wanted to own her own music and the songs she had written herself. And so, in August 2019, Taylor made a big announcement. She was going to rerecord these albums herself. That way, she would own the rights to this new version of the music. She'd add extra tracks and bonuses to encourage her fans to play "Taylor's Version" of the albums instead of the original versions.

COVID Projects

Taylor immediately got started on her rerecording project, and when her *Lover* tour was cut short during the COVID-19 pandemic, Taylor hunkered down at home along with everyone else in the world. The only difference was, she started writing songs for two new albums, which debuted in 2020, *folklore* and *evermore*, featuring Taylor's most indie-pop sound yet.

The Eras Era

From the moment the tour was announced, anticipation for tickets was high – so high that Ticketmaster actually cancelled the public sale of the tickets due to pressure on their systems. In other words, the supply couldn't keep up with the Swifties' demands. Taylor added tour dates, increasing the number of shows from 27 to 52.

Taylor released *Midnights* in October 2022. Then she started training for the tour. She had to be fit to sing and dance for hours every night, so Taylor would run and walk on a treadmill while singing songs from the sets.

FUN FACT

Taylor's first rerecord, *Fearless (Taylor's Version)*, came out in April 2021, and on November 1, 2022, Taylor took to her Instagram with a big, big announcement – she was going on tour again, and this time, she'd be performing songs from aLL of her albums – aLL of her eras, so to speak. World, meet the Eras tour!

READ, READ, READ!

Taylor loves to read and share her favourite authors. Read on for a curated list!

- Daphne du Maurier - This British author wrote the gothic classic *Rebecca*, a novel that inspired one of the songs on *evermore*.

- F. Scott Fitzgerald - Author of the American classic *The Great Gatsby*, which tells the story of love and money in the 1920s.

- Charlotte Brontë -This nineteenth-century author wrote *Jane Eyre*, the gothic tale of a governess who finds love in a lonely English manor.

- E. B. White -Taylor loves *Charlotte's Web*, the ultimate story of a friendship between a pig and a spider.

- John Green - *The Fault in Our Stars* is the story of love between young cancer survivors – and one of Taylor's favourite books.

EASTER EGG HUNT

Taylor loves to hide clues to her music and life for her fans to find. "I think the first time that I started dropping sort of cryptic clues and things in my music was when I was fourteen, fifteen, putting together my first album," Taylor has said. "And I wanted to do something that incentivized fans to read the lyrics." She'd hide secret codes and passages in the liner notes for fans to find. And the tradition has continued ever since.

☆ In 2019, Taylor posted a photo on Instagram of seven palm trees. Her fans quickly figured out that the four trees on one side were her four country albums. The two trees on the other side were her pop albums. And the big tree in the middle ... was her *new* album! Taylor later said that she posted the picture the day she finished *Lover*.

☆ Taylor told fans that they were right when they guessed that the 'William Bowery' on various *folklore* and *evermore* tracks was code for her boyfriend, Joe Alwyn. 'William' was the name of Joe's great-grandfather, and Joe has said that 'Bowery' references an area of New York where he used to hang out.

☆ The day before Taylor announced her ninth album, *evermore*, she tweeted out nine tree emojis.

☆ In Taylor's merch store, there was a signed CD priced at $20.10 – which happens to be the year *Speak Now* came out. And the colour of the font was the exact colour of the *Speak Now* album cover. Taylor was Easter egg-ing the rerelease of *Speak Now* and her fans were there for it!

☆ When Taylor posted a promo for her song 'This Love', in May 2022, she wrote that the song would release at "midnight". *Midnight*, hmm? She even spelled the word "m i d n i g h t" with extra spaces between each letter. Seven months later, her album *Midnights* was released.

And while Taylor used snakes heavily as a symbol of her feud with Kim Kardashian and Kanye West, she also displayed a (fake) back tattoo during the video for 'You Need to Calm Down' (from *Lover*) that depicted a snake turning into a flock of butterflies – an Easter egg hint that Taylor was moving on.

The glamorous dress Taylor wore to the 2024 Grammys made her fans speculate that she was dropping another Easter egg: her white-and-black ensemble recalled the white-and-black feathers of an albatross (a type of sea bird). Was Taylor hinting at the bonus track on *The Tortured Poets Department*, which just happens to be called … 'The Albatross'?

In her video for 'Out of the Woods', from *1989*, Taylor wears a blue dress that looks like the blue dress she was photographed wearing on a yacht while breaking up with Harry Styles. She also rips a paper aeroplane necklace from her neck – the same necklace that Harry often wears. Easter egg alert! 'Out of the Woods' is about Taylor and Harry's relationship.

- In 2021, Taylor teased the start of her rereleases with a clue-filled video referencing "the vault" – all her unreleased songs from *Fearless*.

- A whole year and a half before *Lover* was released, Taylor displayed pastel-painted fingernails during a video for 'Delicate', from *reputation*. She said later that she was calling out *Lover*'s colours - and eventual release.

- Taylor often hides her birth year as an Easter egg, too – in the video for 'I Can See You', from *Speak Now*, when '1989' is visible above a bridge.

- Taylor referenced her dispute with Scooter Braun over her album rights in the video for *Lover*'s 'The Man', when she shows a shot of a grimy sign with an image of a scooter crossed out – that's 'No Scooters' to those of you following along at home.

- Taylor never leaves out thirteen, her favourite number. In her video for *folklore*'s 'Cardigan', the hands of a clock are clearly visible at one and three – thirteen!

She worked out and took three months of dance training so she could feel confident and relaxed on stage.

On March 17, 2023, Taylor kicked off the Eras tour in Glendale, Arizona. It was a gruelling, exhilarating schedule. Each show lasted over three hours, included over 40 songs, multiple costume changes and elaborate stage sets. Each night, ticket sales brought in about $14 million as Taylor played for as many as 96,000 fans. Swifties dressed up in their favourite era clothing, traded friendship bracelets, cried, screamed and danced. At one Massachusetts show, Taylor sang and danced for three and a half hours in the pouring rain. It was so wet that the next night, her soaked piano went haywire and started playing by itself.

In August 2023, Taylor took the Eras tour worldwide. She added another 94 stops – and she's already made over $1 billion, breaking a record held by rock and pop legend Elton John.

But the Eras era wasn't over yet – in October 2023, Taylor released *Taylor Swift: The Eras Tour*, a two hour and forty-five minute concert movie that swept fans inside a series of her Los Angeles shows. So far, the film has made about $260 million.

Travis and Taylor

Meanwhile, Taylor was in another era. Her relationship with the Kansas City Chiefs' tight end Travis Kelce started in July 2023, when Travis made her a friendship bracelet – like a true Swiftie – with his phone number in beads. He wanted to give it to her during an Eras show in Kansas City, Missouri, but didn't get a chance to meet her at the show. Taylor must have got the message somehow, because shortly afterwards, the two went to dinner for their first date. By September, Taylor and Travis were hanging out regularly. Taylor donned a Chiefs jersey and sat in the box during one of Travis's games – and even met his mum.

As their relationship deepened, Taylor went to more and more of Travis's games, bringing friends and her mum. Taylor and Travis appeared on *Saturday Night Live* together, celebrated Halloween, and, in November, Travis flew to Buenos Aires, Argentina, to support Taylor at one of her Eras shows.

At Christmas time, Taylor put on a Christmas hat in the Chiefs box to support Travis, and cheered beside her own brother, Austin. Then, on New Year's Eve, Taylor and Travis gave each other a big kiss at midnight, Travis then gave Taylor a gold bracelet with the initials *T-N-T* – for "Travis and Taylor". He has a matching one for himself. On February 11, Taylor flew back from Tokyo, Japan, where she'd been performing, in time to watch her boyfriend help the Kansas City Chiefs win the Super Bowl.

Taylor's World

With Travis by her side, Taylor has continued to wow the world. In December 2023, she was named *Time* magazine's Person of the Year, honouring her musical and cultural influence, and in February 2024, she won her fourth Album of the Year Grammy for *Midnights*, making her the first person ever to win Album of the Year four times.

Taylor announced her brand-new album, *The Tortured Poets Department* in this speech.

The Tortured Poets Department released on 19th April 2024 and was an instant hit. It broke the record for 'most streamed album' in 24 hours. Just two hours after its release,

Taylor shocked fans with a surprise second batch of songs. This extended album was dubbed *The Anthology*.

This record-breaking album debuted with just over 1.9 million units sold in the US in its first week. The visual aesthetics of the album had a dark academia tone that fans instantly loved. The mid-tempo songs were a fusion of folk-pop, country, rock and synth-pop genres. The critics' reviews, though mixed, were mostly positive. The album was praised for its storytelling, vulnerability and themes of love and loss.

The lead song on the album, 'Fortnight' (featuring Post Malone), an '80s-inspired electropop ballad, rose straight to the top of the charts. The gothic storytelling and the tale of a past relationship won over critics and fans. Taylor directed the video herself and worked with Rodrigo Prieto on the striking cinematography. 'Fortnight' won 'Video of the Year', adding to Taylor's record-breaking list of wins. The video included gothic science themes that echoed *Frankenstein*, featured dramatic lace-filled costumes, and even had surprise appearances from movie stars Ethan Hawke and Josh Charles from The Dead Poets Society.

TTPD won the Top Billboard album and was nominated for many awards such as the Grammy's Album of the Year and the American Music Awards. It also won Global Streaming of 2024 and Global Vinyl Album of 2024. This album broke records in many countries and set records among female artists. "For me, the reward is the work," she said in her Grammy acceptance speech.

New Heights, New Eras

Taylor stunned fans by appearing on her boyfriend Travis Kelce's podcast, *New Heights*.

This special episode, released on August 13, 2025, was eye-opening. Taylor spoke with Travis and his brother Jason Kelce about everything – from her music to the Eras Tour and her relationship with Travis. Fans noticed how comfortable she seemed with Travis and how open she was – it was like seeing another side of Taylor.

During the interview, Taylor said, "I love this new world that Travis has shown me. It's so fun. It's so exciting," showing how happy she felt in their relationship.

She announced a new era and album, instantly breaking the internet. She showed a green and orange suitcase and shared pictures showing this new era. The images were full of glitz and glam, with Taylor's signature red lips, feather boas and lots of glitter. These photos also showed different album covers and vinyl designs.

Engagement announcement

On August 26th 2025, Taylor Swift and Travis Kelce celebrated their two-year relationship and announced their engagement on social media. The photos showed them hugging in a fairy-tale garden full of flowers. The couple captioned their post: 'Your English teacher and your gym teacher are getting married.'

Taylor wore a striped midi dress and her signature red lipstick. The look was an instant hit, just like her music, and fans were eager to replicate it – the dress sold out within 20 minutes of Taylor's post. Her ring caught everyone's attention online and in magazines, praised for its romantic, vintage style. The beautiful yellow gold ring had a big, sparkling 8-carat diamond. It was very valuable, worth between $500,000 and $1 million. Later, it was revealed that Travis helped design the ring, which made fans even more excited.

The announcement took over the world and made headlines. Fans and celebrities rushed to congratulate Taylor and Travis. The post got over 10 million likes in just one hour. That day also set a record: the podcast episode featuring Taylor became the most-viewed live podcast of all time.

Even weeks after the news broke, hype surrounding the wedding hadn't faded. Fans and fashion lovers were wondering about the wedding, and of course, the dress. What will she wear? Who will design her gown? What will be the theme for the wedding?

One thing was certain: the wedding excitement was in the air, and everyone was sharing in the joy of the happy couple.

The Life of a Showgirl

Taylor's latest album, *The Life of a Showgirl*, released on October 2025. Since the announcement on Travis and Jason Kelce's podcast, the anticipation for the album was sky high. The album had a different sound to *The Tortured Poet's Department*, with Taylor returning to her pop sound. Taylor worked with producers Max Martin and Shellback for a more upbeat sound in comparison to the gothic and haunting motifs in TTPD. Unlike previous albums, TLOAS had no bonus tracks, making it Taylor's shortest album. However, the album had 29 different physical versions with alternative covers and two digital variants. The title track features Sabrina Carpenter, who is known for her showgirl aesthetic and was one of the opening acts of the Eras tour.

The album sold 2.7 million copies in the

US on its release day, making it the highest selling album in a single day ... ever. *The Life of a Showgirl* debuted to mixed reviews, although mostly positive. Critics enjoyed the fun rhythms of the production and praised Taylor's pop melodies.

And with a new album released – Taylor enters a glittering new era filled with music, love and joy. As she recently reflected, "I've learned to trust what's coming next, and I'm excited for everything the future holds."

FUN FACT

Taylor's fans make friendship bracelets because of a line in "You're On Your Own, Kid." Often the letters on the bracelets spell out lyrics, quotes, song titles and inside jokes from the Swiftie fandom. At the Eras tour, many fans traded bracelets with one another!

IT'S A LOVE STORY

Taylor's had many relationships over the years – some short, some long and all scrutinized intensely by her fans. Read on for a few details!

- Taylor dated pop star, Joe Jonas, of the Jonas brothers, for only a few months in 2008, and even though the relationship didn't end well (Joe broke up with Taylor on the phone), she still got good song material out of it. 'Forever and Always' from *Fearless* is about Joe.

- Taylor Times Two debuted in autumn of 2009 when Taylor began dating actor Taylor Lautner. Taylor wrote 'Back to December', from *Speak Now*, about her time with the other Taylor, and today, the two Taylors remain friends.

Singer John Mayer and Taylor stepped out for a few months from December 2009 to February 2010. Was John mean to Taylor? Swift fans have asked this question online repeatedly. From the stage, Taylor has urged them to be kind.

Taylor and actor Jake Gyllenhaal dated from October 2010 to January 2011, and Taylor wrote several songs on *Red* about Jake. The couple spent time together in Nashville and Los Angeles before their relationship ended.

Taylor and singer Harry Styles had a relationship that lasted from about October 2012 to January 2013. Taylor wore Harry's silver aeroplane necklace, and the two hung out at New York's Central Park Zoo. Taylor wrote many of the tunes on *1989* about Harry, and Harry said later that he didn't mind being her inspiration for such great songs.

Sparks flew when Taylor met Scottish DJ Calvin Harris at the *Elle* Style Awards in February 2015, and the two began their own "Love Story". By the time the relationship ended in March 2016, Taylor and Calvin had been going out for over a year.

Taylor briefly dated British actor Tom Hiddleston in the summer of 2016, but soon she was in a serious relationship with another British actor, Joe Alwyn. Taylor wanted to keep this relationship as quiet as possible, so she and Joe hid out and avoided the paparazzi. Taylor and Joe were together for six years, until 2023, when they quietly broke up, saying that their relationship had just run its course.

Taylor and Kansas City Chiefs football player Travis Kelce have been together since July 2023 when Travis made Taylor a friendship bracelet with his phone number on it. In February 2024, Taylor was in the stands to watch Travis and the Chiefs win that year's Super Bowl.

A TAYLOR TIMELINE

December 13, 1989

Taylor is born in Reading, Pennsylvania.

1999–2000

Taylor starts singing in local karaoke competitions.

2002

Taylor learns how to play guitar. She sings the National Anthem at a Philadelphia 76ers game, wowing the crowd with her beautiful voice.

2003

Taylor and her family move to Nashville from Pennsylvania so she can pursue her dream of becoming a country music star.

2006

'Tim McGraw' is released as Taylor's debut single. Taylor records and releases her first album, *Taylor Swift*.

2007

Taylor accepts her first major music award, the Horizon Award, at the Country Music Association Awards.

2008

Taylor releases *Fearless*, her first number one record.

2009

Fearless becomes the year's bestselling album. Taylor wins her first Album of the Year Grammy. 'You Belong with Me' becomes Taylor's crossover country-to-pop single. Taylor wins the Moonman Award for Best Female Video, but her acceptance speech is interrupted by Kanye West.

2010

Speak Now comes out.

2012

Taylor drops her fourth album, *Red*.

2013

Taylor opens the Taylor Swift Education Centre at the Country Music Hall of Fame in Nashville.

2014

1989 is released.

2015

The *1989* world tour breaks the record for the highest grossing U.S. tour by a female artist. Taylor's mum, Andrea, is diagnosed with breast cancer.

2017

Taylor returns to public life with the release of her sixth album, *reputation*, which becomes the best selling album of the year.

2018

Taylor takes *reputation* on tour with stagecraft featuring snakes. She breaks her silence on political issues,encouraging her fans to register to vote in the mid-term elections.

2019

Taylor releases her seventh album, *Lover*. The album promotion and tour are cut short by the COVID-19 pandemic.

2020

folklore is released as Taylor's eighth studio album, followed by evermore, the ninth album, both recorded during COVID lockdown. Taylor also starts rerecording some of her earlier albums.

2021

Fearless (Taylor's Version) and *Red (Taylor's Version)* are released.

2022

Midnights, Taylor's tenth studio album, is released. She announces the Eras tour. Ticketmaster crashes due to the overwhelming demand.

2023

The Eras tour kicks off in Glendale, Arizona. Taylor releases *Speak Now (Taylor's Version)*, *1989 (Taylor's Version)* and *Taylor Swift: The Eras Tour* concert film. Taylor is ranked by *Forbes* magazine as the fifth most powerful woman in the world. In December, Taylor is named *Time* magazine's Person of the Year.

2024

Taylor wins her fourth Grammy for Album of the Year, making her the first musician to win that prize four times. Taylor also released her eleventh album, *The Tortured Poets Department*.

2025

Taylor announces her engagement to Travis Kelce on August. Her twelfth album, *The Life of a Showgirl* released in October and topped the charts.